MOXIE DAY
and Family

A Laugh and Learn Book of Poetry

Hooray for Moxie Day! Robert Pottle has done it again, and this time you're going to love being bitten by the Poetry Bug. Learning about poetry has never been so much fun.

-Kenn Nesbitt, author of *The Aliens Have Landed!*

Moxie Day is a perfect blend of truth and humor. A delightful read for both the young and the young at heart.

-Linda Knaus, children's poet

This book boldly brings together fun and learning. In his second published work, Robert Pottle, with the help of Poetry Bug, Fly Guy, and the Day family, takes readers on a playful, month by month journey into the wonderful world of poetry. Children will love the humorous poems and the comic strips that accompany them. Teachers will be inspired to develop lessons that have their students immersed in the often forgotten literary craft of verse.

-Jim Cliffe, 3rd grade teacher

MOXIE DAY

and Family

A Laugh and Learn Book of Poetry

poems by
Robert Pottle

illustrations by
Jonathan Siruno

Blue Lobster Press

MOXIE DAY and Family
Text Copyright © 2002 by Robert Pottle
Illustration Copyright © 2002 by Jonathan Siruno

ISBN 0-9709569-1-6

For Miss Libby. You earned it.

-R.P.

For Samantha and Jen-Jen (who baked me a birthday cake during Thanksgiving, even though my birthday is in December), for being real Moxie Days.

-J.S.

Acknowledgments

Thank you, Diane, for reading numerous bad drafts of poems and being politely honest. I offer apologies for the many times my mind wandered off mid-conversation during the writing of this book as I internally debated whether the word 'smooching' or 'hugging' was funnier. Thank you, to my family, my mother, who instilled a love of children's literature in me; my father, who shared a passion for poking fun at children's literature; and my brother, who at times drove me crazy growing up, but provided a lot of material to write about in the process. Even if Leigh Beatty didn't help edit this book, I'd have to thank her for being one of the kindest people I know. Thank you, Leigh. Thank you, to my teachers and professors, in particular, Don Canton, Bill Roorbach and Wesley McNair. Thank you, for encouraging me as a writer and for your honest critiques. And lastly, thank you, Shel Silverstein, for writing books that were funny, honest, and appropriately irreverent.

- R.P.

First and foremost, I'd like to thank my parents for all the support they've given me, even when I decided to go to art school to be a funnybook artist instead of a doctor. I also have to thank my sister April for being a sounding board and my own little cheerleader squad. An eternal debt of gratitude goes out to the proud members of the Atomic Underpants Studios (Les, Nate, Ryan, Steve and Andrew) and all my artist friends, who know when to be brutally honest and when to lie to me when I need an ego boost. And finally, I have to thank my elementary school art teacher Mr. Cote, who set the foundation for my artistic career.

- J.S.

Introduction #1
For kids only! Parents and teachers don't read, see below.

This is a funny book, but some adults might not like the humor. It's about broken zippers, misbehaving in school, and pulling pranks on your family. It even makes fun of teachers! Best of all, you can talk your parents and teachers into buying this book! Here's what you say: "(Insert adult's name here), I've always wanted to enrich myself by learning more about poetry. I've just found the only kids book ever written that explains 26 poetic terms like, clerihew, cinquain, and double dactyl. It even has over 80 frames of sequential art. Could you please help me on my quest for self-enrichment by getting this book?" Before you know it, you'll be laughing at characters like Meathead and Captain Cootie. By the way, sequential art means comic strip, but don't tell the adults.

Introduction #2
For adults only! Kids don't read, see above.

Would you like your children to be well-rounded individuals? Do you want your children to experience fine art forms such as poetry and sequential art? This book will expose children to a wide variety of poetic forms, and define numerous poetic terms. It even includes over 80 frames of sequential art. There has never been another book like it. Best of all, children will love this book. They'll read it over and over again. They'll share it with their friends. They'll develop an appreciation for art and literature that will last a lifetime. When your children are grown, and accepting Pulitzer and Nobel prizes, you'll thank yourself for enriching their lives with fine literature such as this. By the way, I also have a used car for sale, call if interested.

DADDY DAY
will often say
a thing or two
that isn't true.

MAMA DAY
will often pray
for just one night
the kids won't fight.

MURPHY DAY
nothing goes his way;
a lucky charm
could cause him harm.

MEATHEAD
is well fed;
he runs like a flash
to eat from the trash.

Wiggledy Giggledy
Little Miss Moxie Day,
pest to her teacher and
family, but

school kids all laugh at her
hyperhysterically
when she acts out like a
lunatic nut.

September

The First Day of Kindergarten	Moxie
Black Beard	Murphy
Ouch!	Murphy
Bak too Skool	Murphy

The First Day of
Kindergarten

Today was it. I went to school.
It was fun and kinda cool.
We did the hokey-pokey dance.
Peter cried; he wet his pants.
Miss Libby said to make a line.
I got paper. I drew mine.
But all the kids were in a row.
Miss Libby said, "Come on, let's go."
I sang and drew and had some fun.
I've gone to school and now I'm done.

Huh?
What did you say?
I've got to go another day?
I am not done this afternoon?
I've got to go until mid-June!
I thought today I was all done.
I guess today was just day one.

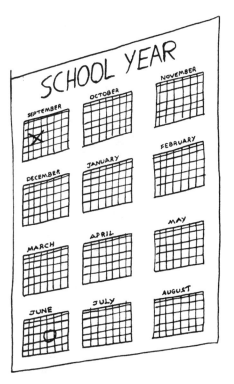

Black Beard

He angrily barks out his orders.
His face wears a permanent scowl.
And if you should ask him a question
his only response is to growl.

His discipline methods are ruthless.
He believes in all work and no play.
And if you should happen to step out of line
it may be with your life you will pay.

I'd rather an octopus hug me.
I'd rather have sharks bite my rear
than to walk into class on the first day of school
to find Black Beard's my teacher this year.

Ouch!

Meathead is our family dog.
Boy, he sure is dumb.
He never has retrieved a stick.
He hides when we yell, "Come. "

Meathead is a friendly dog.
He plays with friends of mine.
Once when walking in the woods
we met a porcupine.

Meathead ran and wagged his tail,
off to make a friend.
I ran to try and stop him
'cause I knew how that would end.

I finally got between them
and I hollered, "Meathead, sit!"
But Meathead charged full speed ahead;
he wasn't going to quit.

I raised my arms as Meathead jumped.
I wobbled when I caught him...

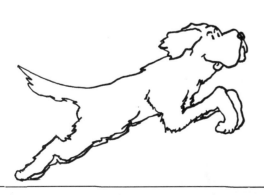

...then fell on to the porcupine,
and quills stuck in my bottom.

Bak too Skool

I kan spel dae
and I kan spel nite.
I kan spel just abowt
evreething rite!

And fore werdz I doent noe
like noomoenya
      nat
      nee
I just get a dikshunairee
kuz thair I wil see
tha rite wae too spel it,
tha letrz too uze.
See, speling iz eezee;
I doent bloe a fuze.

Its eezee too spel.
Its eezee I sed.
Its eezee too spel
if yoo just uze yore hed!

October

The Store	Moxie
Sharing	Moxie
Scary Costume	Moxie
On Halloween	Moxie

The Store

You can cash in your coupons for cooties.
Strange smells will sell for a cent.
You can purchase your pimples for pennies,
Or, if you'd prefer, you may rent.

Lanky limbs sell for a dollar.
Greasy hair goes for a dime.
The clothes that I sell are the coolest,
'cause they're colored bright orange and lime.

See, my cousin has just started high school,
and he says that he's stylish and in.
So, I'm starting a store for all people
who wish to be stylish like him.

Sharing

Miss Libby says to share the toys
with all the other girls and boys.
I have to share the rubber duck,
the plastic phone, the yellow truck.
I have to share the baby doll,
the boat, the books, the bouncy ball.
I'll tell you what I'd like to do;
I'd like to share the stomach flu.
Then all the kids would stay at home,
and I could play here all alone.

ALONE AND HOME
ARE AN EXAMPLE OF
ASSONANT RHYME.
CATCH ME AT THE
END TO LEARN MORE.

Scary Costume

With an evil eye that can stop you cold,
and a bulbous warty nose,
a furrowed brow, a nasty scowl,
and old out-dated clothes,
my costume is the scariest
the world has ever seen.
I'm not an ogre, ghost, or ghoul;
I'm a teacher for Halloween.

On Halloween

On Halloween, Frankenstein
    came to our door.
Mom didn't know he was real.

She gave him one gumball
    and not any more.
Then Frankenstein said, "Here's the deal.

"I'm Frankenstein, ma'am,
    and I've come to this town
to be mean 'cause I'm in a bad mood.

"I'll scare you, then chase you,
    then tear your house down."
Mom scolded and said, "Don't be rude."

Then Frankenstein growled
    and said things that weren't kind.
Then Mom grabbed a broom used for sweeping.

She swung with that broom
    to swat his behind,
and Frankenstein ran away weeping!

November

November 1st	Moxie
Art Class	Moxie
Follow-the-Leader	Moxie
Mom!	Murphy

November 1st

Dial China on the phone.
Steal your brother's ice cream cone;
use the microwave to boil it.
Flush the car keys down the toilet.

Prance and dance. Skip and dip.
Tango, fandango, disco, flip.
Eat bananas. Eat the peels.
Bark like twenty singing seals.

Sing out silly, loud and long.
Sing a hard rock opera song.
To terrorize your dads and moms,
eat eighty super-sugar bombs.

Art Class

Icky pooh, sticky glue,
stuck on me and stuck on you.
Glue in my hair, but I don't care.
It's on my face and everywhere.

My little toe's stuck to my nose.
Guess that's just the way it goes
with icky pooh, sticky glue,
stuck on me and stuck on you.

Trouble comes when we touch thumbs.
Guess we'll have to call our moms,
'cause icky pooh, sticky glue,
you're stuck to me, and me to you.

THIS TYPE OF STANZA IS CALLED A QUATRAIN. LEARN MORE WITH ME AT THE END OF THE BOOK.

Follow-the-Leader

Don't see what's so fun about follow-the-leader.
First it was Katie, then David, now Peter.
Peter is leading us all down the hall.
What's worse is he's going to make all of us crawl.
Crawling's for babies. It isn't for me.
Ow! I've got rug burns all over my knee.
Now Kimberly's first. What is she doing?
I feel so embarrassed. She's got us all mooing.
Of all the dumb games, I like this one the worst.
I'm quitting. I'm leaving. I'll never...

What's that?

It's my turn to be first!

Did I happen to mention that I love this game
when me and the leader are one and the same.

Mom!

Where's my Captain Cootie first edition comic book?
I've looked in every single place that's sensible to look.
I keep the comic hidden in the dresser with my socks,
sealed inside an acid-free, airtight, cardboard box.
That comic never has been touched or seen the light of day.
Whoever took my comic book is gonna hafta pay.
I'll peek into my sister's room; she always takes my stuff.
But this is where I draw the line and say enough's enough.

I hope that what I'm seeing's an illusion or mirage.
My sister cut The Captain out to use in her collage!

December

Why Do I Have to
    Learn to Count Money?   Daddy
The True Meaning of Christmas   Moxie
When Santa Came to School   Moxie
Mistletoe Millie   Moxie

Why Do I Have to Learn to Count Money?

If you learn to count money before you get tall,
you can work in the ATM down at the mall.
The boy inside now is getting too large,
so learn to count quick and they'll put you in charge.
Listen to me 'cause I always know why.
I know it all, and of course I don't lie.

The True Meaning of Christmas

At church they asked what Christmas meant.
I knew that. Up my hand went.
When I was asked, I said with glee,
"On that day I get gifts. You see,
my family loves me - I'm so great -
they buy me gifts to celebrate."
At least that's how it seems to me.
The preacher seemed to disagree.

When Santa Came to School

Santa came and said to me,
"Have you been good? Now let me see."
He checked his list, then he frowned
and groaned a deep, depressing sound.
But still he said, "Speak loud and clear
and tell me what you want this year."
I said, "I told you yesterday."
He looked confused, to my dismay.
I said, "Remember, at the mall?"
He cleared his throat and tried to stall.
Then his face turned bright and red.
"I can't remember," Santa said.
"Well, what I want," I said to him…

but I forgot. Now things look grim
'cause here it is half past December
and what I want we can't remember!

Mistletoe Millie

The whole family's gathered
and Mistletoe Millie
is kissing and smooching
and acting all silly.
She got Grampie Zeke
and kissed him on the cheek.
She caught Cousin Flynn
and kissed him on the chin.
She found Mr. Fips
and kissed him on the lips!
She ran up to me...

...but I figured it out;
I held up our dog,
which she kissed on the snout.
She found it so gross
that she fell on the floor.
Guess she won't try
to kiss me anymore.

41

January

I Think I'll Leave
    My Snowsuit On   Murphy
Show and Tell   Moxie
The Prank   Murphy
Grammar Lesson   Murphy

I Think I'll Leave My Snowsuit On

Last night I didn't sleep so well.
I tossed and turned all night.
This morning I was snoring loud
and drooling, what a sight.
Woke up to see the bus outside,
waiting in the snow.
My sister said, "Hey, snore-o-saur,
come on, it's time to go!"
Put on my snowsuit, boots, and hat
in a hurry scurry dance.
Got to school, my face turned red;
I forgot to put on pants!

Show and Tell

This is my bear. His name is Gray.
I give him loving everyday.
But so much love has worn him down.
He once was gray, but now he's brown.
His old left leg is barely on.
His eye fell off. Now it's gone.
His ear was ripped, but now it's patched.
His button nose came unattached.
Mama had to fix his head.
She looked at Gray, sighed and said,
"This type of love is fine for Gray;
just hope I don't get loved this way."

46

The Prank

Two snacks upon the table,
one for Moxie, one for me.
I think it's time that I went on
a little eating spree.

I'll gobble hers, then swallow mine,
and it will make me glad,
to be the one for a change,
making someone mad.

Chunky, crunchy, grainy, gritty,
a little hard to chew,
these snacks have made my breath smell like
a trash can or a shoe.

Moxie comes into the room.
I'm prepared if she attacks.
Instead, she laughs at me, and says...

"You just ate doggy snacks!"

Grammar Lesson

Oh, teacher, I fear that I misunderstood
whether I should use well, or if I should use good.
If roses had noses then how would they smell?
Would they smell good or would they smell well?

February

What Really Happened
 to the Unicorns?   *Daddy*
Getting Out   *Murphy*
Haiku   *Murphy*
Paying Attention   *Moxie*

What Really Happened to the Unicorns?

You know when Noah was a floatin' way on out in the sea,
he was savin' all the creatures, so they could be free.
And here's a little somethin' that you may not have heard,
but my story is the truth, I give you my word.

Spend forty days at sea and you're bound to get thinner,
especially when raw fish is all you're havin' for dinner.
After thirty days of floatin' Noah said, "No more fish.
Tonight I'm gonna have me somethin' else on my dish."

So, Noah was a-starvin' as he walked 'round the ship
and gazed upon each creature with a smack of his lip.
He eyed a hog, a dog, a platypus, but sure as you're born,
the tastiest of them all was the Unicorn.

Getting Out

Button, button, Velcro, snap,
puffy coat and woolly cap.
A dozen strings that must be tied.
All this work to go outside.

Zipper, zipper, fasten, click,
smelly boots make me sick.
Try ten times to tie a knot.
The weather's cool, boots are not.

Tugging, pulling, buckle, belt,
run outside before I melt.
When I finally hit the snow...
Emergency! I have to go!

Haiku

Snow bending the boughs
finally falls from the tree
and lands on my face.

THIS FORM OF
POETRY IS A HAIKU.
WHAT IS A HAIKU?
FLIP TO THE BACK
TO LEARN MORE.

Paying Attention

Sometimes I like to sit and think
of weird and wacky things,
like goats with capes
and coats for grapes
and phones with wedding rings.

Then other times I lie around
and have the oddest thoughts,
where clowns made kings
wed worms with wings
that tie themselves in knots.

Then when I have to concentrate,
my mind will get all funny,
and chocolate rains
on subway planes
and the moon is dipped in honey.

The worlds that wander through my mind
are worlds that don't exist.
But there's not one
that isn't fun,
so how can I resist?

March

Our Dog   Murphy
Picture Day   Moxie
Funny Time   Moxie
Embarrassed   Murphy

Our Dog

Our dog eats from the garbage can
    and stirs up quite a stink.
Our dog eats from the garbage can,
    then goes to get a drink.
Our dog drinks from the toilet bowl,
    disgusting but it's true.
Our dog drinks from the toilet bowl,
    an awful thing to do.
Our dog's a very friendly dog,
    although he's kinda thick.
Our dog's a very friendly dog, but...
    his kisses make me sick.

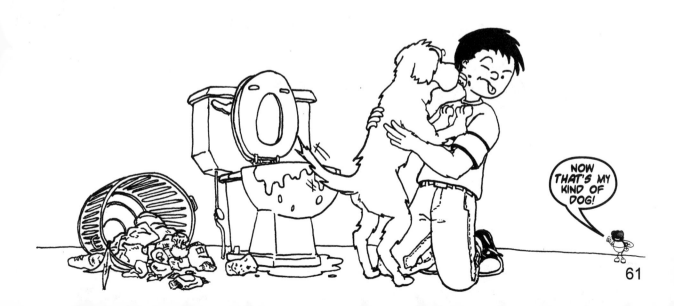

Picture Day

My parents thought I should look nice. They dressed me in a gown.
But in that dress I get depressed, so all I did was frown.

FLASH

Mom thought a snack might make me smile. I had a lemon sucker.
When I was done my dad said, "Smile." All I could do was pucker.

FLASH

Then they said to have a seat in the comfy chair.
On the way I scuffed my feet for spiky static hair.

FLASH

I'd tried for years with no success, so imagine my surprise,
when my father snapped the shot I learned to cross my eyes!

FLASH

My father said, "Get this one right, or else I'll have you hung."
I thought the picture would look best if I stuck out my tongue.

FLASH

When I made those faces, I meant it as a joke,
but now my father's really mad because the camera's broke.

Funny Time

Went up to the rooftop. I brought the kitchen clock,
wound up like a pitcher, and threw it 'cross the block.
Then I giggled, snickered, laughed, with Mama's watch in hand.
I threw her watch so forcefully, I bet it didn't land.
My mother doesn't seem to laugh. I don't know why she cries.
I heard her say, just yesterday, "It's funny how time flies."

Embarrassed

My zipper is broken.
There's bound to be jokin'
and normally I wouldn't care.
But today was the day,
I am sorry to say,
I forgot to put on underwear.

WELL, MAYBE
THIS POEM IS
OKAY. YEAH,
IT'S FUNNY.

April

At the Farm	Moxie
April Fools	Moxie
Running Away	Moxie
The Artist	Moxie

At the Farm

I heard a rabbit go, "oink oink."
I heard a duck go, "moo."
I heard a pig out in the mud
go, "cock-a-doodle-doo."

I'm sure I heard the horses quack,
and then the roosters neigh.
"Old MacDonald Had a Farm"
was never sung this way.

The sounds these creatures ought to make
are taught in all the schools,
but disregard those lessons learned;
today is April Fool's!

April Fools

I wanted to make a prank call,
but since I'm not allowed
to use the phone anymore,
I decided to write a prank
letter instead.

Dear Sir, Is your refrigerator running? Please
respond.

And he did:
Dear Ma'am, Thank you for the note;
after reading it I turned
to see my refrigerator running
away. It would have escaped,
but bumped its head on the door
and knocked itself cold.
By the way, is your nose running?

Immediately I wrote back
to tell him that he could not
fool me
with my own clever trick.
Then I wiped my nose, just to check.
It was gone!

70

Running Away

I'm running away and I'm leaving tonight.
My parents and I, we got into a fight.
They said at the table I couldn't be rude.
They said that I wasn't allowed to throw food!
So, I'm packing my things and I won't bring a comb.
I'll wear my hair messy wherever I roam.
I won't bring my toothbrush, my shampoo, or floss.
I won't listen to grown-ups. I'll be my own boss.
I'm leaving. Don't stop me. Now don't even try.
I'm leaving. Don't stop me. Don't even say bye.
I'll run away far 'cause this isn't a bluff.

SLAM

I think running away to the porch is enough.

The Artist

From drawing blue bananas,
my marker has gone dry.
I'll use my mouth to moisten it
and give another try.

My marker's working better now.
And wow, I love the taste.
It's surprisingly more flavorful
than crayons, chalk, or paste!

Katie starts to giggle.
I ask, "What's wrong with you?"
She points at me, laughs and says,
"Your tongue is colored blue!"

My tongue is blue! How cool is that?
I'm artistic and it shows.
I grab a green, open it,
and color on my nose.

Then with purple, pink, and gray,
yellow, brown, and red,
I color ears and eyes and teeth;
I'm Mrs. Rainbow Head!

Miss Libby looks and throws a fit:
"Why can't you just be good?"
It's hard to be an artist
when you're so misunderstood.

May

Field Trip	Moxie
Shoe Tying	Murphy
Thank You, Captain Cootie	Murphy
Super Spy	Moxie

Field Trip

I need to find a large toothpick.
Or better yet, a ten-foot stick.
I need it for my classmate, Keith,
who's stuck between some walrus teeth.

Shoe Tying

Listen up. I've got some news.
I just hate to tie my shoes.
Monday was completely messed,
tied my shoes before I dressed.
Of course, I took them off, and then
got dressed and tied them up again.

At school a kid stepped on my lace
and made me fall right on my face.
My lace got caught up on the slide,
tore off my shoe. Oh, what a ride.
Seems I'm always tying shoes,
and tying shoes gives me the blues.

When I got home at half past two
I got my father's super glue.
Glue could make those laces stick.
I thought three drops would do the trick.
I ran and played and had some fun;
my shoes were tied when I was done!

Then eight o' clock was time for bed.
At least that's what my parents said.
At last I could untie those shoes,
but once again I had the blues.
I found my mother, then I cried,
"I can't get my shoes untied!"

THIS TYPE OF STANZA
IS CALLED A SIXAIN.
CATCH UP WITH ME IN
THE BACK OF THE BOOK
TO FIND OUT WHY.

Thank You, Captain Cootie

Ripped my pants at school today
while going down the slide.
It wasn't just a little tear;
I ripped 'em open wide.

Now all can see my Captain Cootie
purple underwear.
Although The Captain makes some laugh,
I'm glad I've got him there.

Super Spy

He has eyes that see through walls
and ears that hear my thoughts.
He watches me 'bout every day;
it ties my gut in knots.
I'd like to take his spying head
and shove it in a pail,
'cause no one likes - especially me -
the classroom tattle-tale.

June

Play Ball!   Murphy
Tomato Soup   Moxie
The Rubber Band Game   Moxie
Magic Show   Murphy

Play Ball!

The dugout's where I get to play
when baseball season's here.
For basketball I play the bench.
Sometimes I get to cheer.
For golf I get to caddy clubs.
They say I should have fun.
At soccer sideline standing
I'm the best, bar none.
Perhaps it's 'cause I'm clumsy,
or maybe 'cause I'm small;
in any case, when playing sports
I never touch the ball.

Tomato Soup

When Meathead came into the house
we all yelled, "Oh my gosh!"
Tomato soup soon filled the sink
to give our dog a wash.

He reeked like rotten sauerkraut,
mixed with moldy funk.
Meathead had been scented
by a smellorific skunk.

After scrubbing Meathead clean,
it seemed like such a waste
to let that soup go down the drain;
I thought, "How would it taste?"

Tomato soup is something
that my brother likes to eat.
So, I filled a bowl and placed it
on the table by his seat.

The Rubber Band Game

Let's play a game called pull the band.
See, you hold this end in your hand.
I'll take this end - stretch it tight -
now we pull with all our might.
Then I let go and watch the band
as it snaps back and stings your hand.
My, what a lot of pain you're in.
Would you like to play again?

Magic Show

I'm going to a magic show.
There is a trick I hear they know.
So I'll go with my sister dear
and hope they make her disappear.

July

Going   Moxie
The Train Name Game   Moxie
Time to Go   Moxie
Why Does the Moon Follow Me?   Daddy

Going

To go
to grandma's house
we drive a hundred miles.
We stop each time I yell, "I have
to go!"

THIS FORM OF POETRY IS CALLED A *CINQUAIN*. I'LL EXPLAIN OUT BACK.

The Train Name Game

If we went crazy on this train,
then it would be a coo-coo train.

And if some flies filled up the train,
it would become a shoo-shoo train.

If ballerinas rode the train,
then I'd call this a tutu train.

And if a cow came on the train,
why we'd be on a moo-moo train.

Or if babies filled the train,
then this would be a goo-goo train.

And if we fell while on the train,
then we'd be on a boo-boo train.

But since we're eating on this train,
I guess it's just a chew-chew train.

A POEM WITH A SHAPE THAT RESEMBLES SOMETHING IS CALLED *EMBLEMATIC*. HEAD OUT BACK TO LEARN MORE.

Time to Go

My little baby cousin, Piper,
does her business in a diaper.
To tell the truth, I must confess
she makes an awful stinky mess.
And brother doesn't seem to know
exactly where he ought to go.
Last night my brother wet his bed.
"It must have rained," he woke and said.
But beds and diapers aren't for me.
I like to go behind a tree.

OKAY, I ADMIT IT, I LIKE THIS POEM TOO.

YUCK, YOU WOULD LIKE THAT ONE.

Why Does the Moon Follow Me?

The moon in the sky's out to getcha, ya know.
And that's why it follows wherever you go.
See, when you stand here at the edge of the park,
the moon up above watches you through the dark.

And now that we're home, look up; there's the moon.
It's after you, Moxie, and may get you soon
'cause the moon steals all children who don't behave well
and turns them to stars with a magical spell.

So keep one eye open and don't snooze too deep;
the moon does its work in the night when you sleep.
You know I'd protect you if only I could,
but the moon's sure to get you, unless you are good.

Listen to me 'cause I always know why.
I know it all, and of course I don't lie.

August

Good Morning	*Moxie*
We Could Have Bought a Hamster	*Mama*
Poetry	*Moxie*
Laughing	*Moxie*

Good Morning

I'm feeling awful mad today.
I think I should be bad today.
I'll make my parents mad today,
at least as mad as me.

I'll paint the windows black, and then
mix sugar with the salt, and then
I'll make my brother cry, and then
they'll send me to my room.

Then I'll get feeling even worse.
So I'll start acting even worse.
Till mom and dad think I'm the worst
daughter in the world.

We Could Have Bought a Hamster

We could have bought a hamster.
We could have bought a cat.
We could have bought a silent snake;
oh, just imagine that!

We could have bought a lizard,
a llama or a frog.
I think I'd even settle for
another stupid dog.

But someone said he knew a way
to fill our lives with joy.
He said, "Let's start a family
with a little girl and boy."

Now almost every single night
our home's filled with the sound
of screams and shouts and cries and pouts
that come from all around.

We could have bought a hamster.
We could have bought a cat.
We could have bought a silent snake;
oh, just imagine that!

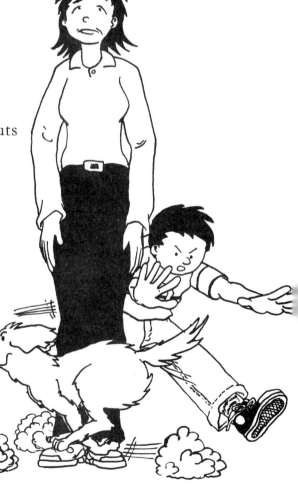

Poetry

Maple syrup comes from a tree
and honey from a honey bee.
Seafood comes out of the sea.
So, what of use comes out of me?

Songs, and laughs, and poetry.

Laughing

Giggle, giggle, snicker, laugh.
Giggle till you split in half.
Chortle-snort and chortle-roar;
laugh and roll around the floor.

Roll and rollick. Jump for joy.
Hoot and holler, boy, oh, boy.
Laugh until you start to cry.
Laugh until you almost die.

Take a breath, then start again;
giggle till 'bout half-past ten.
Laugh until you start to cough.
Laugh until your head falls off.

Laughing helps us to rejoice,
so laugh until you lose your voice.
Now you can't laugh anymore,
so sleep and make a silly snore.

Laugh and Learn with
The Poetry Bug

Stanzas	106
Cinquain	108
Haiku	110
Free Verse	112
Clerihew	113
Double Dactyl	114
Mad Song Stanza	116
Emblematic Verse	117
Perfect Rhyme/Assonant Rhyme	118
Alliteration	119

CINQUAIN

Snow bending the boughs

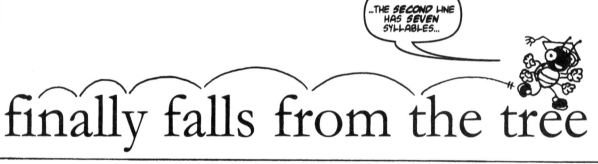

finally falls from the tree

and lands on my face.

FREE VERSE

CLERIHEW

AN *EPIGRAM* IS A SHORT HUMOROUS POEM THAT IS OFTEN USED TO POKE FUN, OR TEASE.

POKE FUN AND TEASE, THOSE ARE TWO OF MY *FAVORITE* THINGS TO DO!

THE INTRODUCTIONS IN THIS BOOK ARE TWO DIFFERENT TYPES OF EPIGRAMS. THE FIRST IS A CLERIHEW, A FORM OF POETRY CREATED BY E. *CLERIHEW BENTLEY*

CLERIHEW? THESE POETS HAVE THE WEIRDEST NAMES.

A CLERIHEW HAS *FOUR* LINES, WHICH MAKES IT A *QUATRAIN*.

THE *FIRST TWO* LINES RHYME WITH EACH OTHER, AS DO THE *LAST TWO* LINES.

THE LINES CAN *VARY* IN THE NUMBER OF *SYLLABLES*.

DADDY DAY
will often say
a thing or two
that isn't true.

MAMA DAY
will often pray
for just one night
the kids won't fight.

THE *FIRST* LINE OF THE POEM IS ALWAYS A *PERSON'S NAME* AND IT IS WRITTEN IN ALL *CAPITAL LETTERS*. THIS IS ALSO THE *TITLE* OF THE POEM.

DADDY DAY
will often say

SO HERE IT GOES, A CLERIHEW BY FLY GUY:

POETRY BUG WILL MAKE YOU GO, "UGH." WHEN HE STARTS TO BLABBER ABOUT SOME POEM, YOU WILL WISH THAT YOU DIDN'T KNOW HIM.

DOUBLE DACTYL

ANOTHER TYPE OF EPIGRAM IS A *DOUBLE DACTYL*. A DOUBLE DACTYL IS FUN TO READ AND CHALLENGING TO WRITE. *ANTHONY HECHT* CREATED THIS FORM OF POETRY.

WHERE DO THESE POETS GET THESE *NAMES*? CRAPSY, CLERIHEW, HECHT.

A DOUBLE DACTYL IS MADE UP OF *TWO QUATRAINS*. EACH OF THE *FIRST THREE LINES* OF THE QUATRAINS HAS *SIX SYLLABLES*.

Wiggledy Giggledy
Little Miss Moxie Day,
pest to her *teacher* and
family, *but*

school kids all *laugh* at her
hyperhysterically
when she acts *out* like a
lunatic nut.

THE *FIRST* AND *FOURTH* SYLLABLES IN EACH OF THESE LINES ARE STRESSED, WHICH MEANS IT IS SPOKEN MORE *FORCEFULLY* THAN THE OTHER SYLLABLES.

THE *FOURTH* AND *EIGHTH* LINE IN BOTH QUATRAINS HAS ONLY *FOUR SYLLABLES*.

Wiggledy Giggledy
Little Miss Moxie Day,
pest to her teacher and
family, but

school kids all laugh at her
hyperhysterically
when she

AGAIN THE STRESS IS ON THE *FIRST* AND *FOURTH* SYLLABLES.

lunatic nut.

NOW, THE *FIRST LINE* OF THE POEM IS ALWAYS TWO *THREE-SYLLABLE WORDS*. OFTEN TIMES THE WORDS HIGGLEDY PIGGLEDY ARE USED, BUT NOT ALWAYS.

Wiggledy Giggledy
Little Miss Moxie Day,
pest to her teacher and
family, but

school kids all laugh at her
hyperhysterically
wh... out like a
lu...

GEE, MY *PARENTS* DIDN'T EVEN HAVE *THIS* MANY RULES.

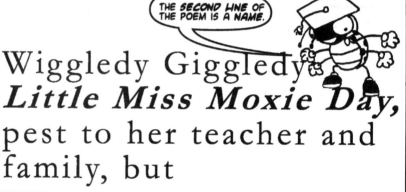

THE *SECOND LINE* OF THE POEM IS A *NAME*.

Wiggledy Giggledy
Little Miss Moxie Day,
pest to her teacher and
family, but

AND FINALLY, EITHER THE *SIXTH* OR *SEVENTH LINE* OF THE POEM MUST BE A SINGLE DESCRIPTIVE *SIX-SYLLABLE WORD*. THIS WORD MUST HAVE THE *FIRST* AND *FOURTH* SYLLABLES STRESSED.

Little Miss...
...st to her teacher a...
...ly, but

...ool kids all laugh at her
hyperhysterically
when sh... out like a
lunatic ...

HOLY COW, THIS FORM OF POETRY HAS MORE *RULES* THAN A *CLASSROOM!*

MAD SONG STANZA

A MAD SONG STANZA HAS FIVE LINES, WHICH MAKES IT A CINQUAIN.

Sometimes I like to sit and think
of weird and wacky things,
like goats with capes
and coats for grapes
and phones with wedding rings.

LINES ONE, TWO, AND FIVE HAVE SIX SYLLABLES*...

...AND LINES THREE AND FOUR HAVE FOUR SYLLABLES.

THE FIRST LINE DOES NOT NEED TO RHYME WITH ANY OTHER LINE...

... BUT LINES TWO AND FIVE RHYME WITH EACH OTHER...

...AS DO LINES THREE AND FOUR.

A MAD SONG STANZA POEM USUALLY SOUNDS LIKE IT IS BEING TOLD BY SOMEONE WHO IS A LITTLE BIT LOONY.

SPEAKING OF A LITTLE BIT LOONY, WHERE DID THAT FLY GUY GO?

*THE POEM IN THIS EXAMPLE IS A VARIATION OF A MAD SONG STANZA BECAUSE THE FIRST LINE HAS EIGHT SYLLABLES.

EMBLEMATIC VERSE

ALLITERATION

You can cash in your coupons for cooties.

You can cash in your coupons for cooties.

Title Index

April Fools	70
Art Class	30
At the Farm	69
Bak too Skool	17
Black Beard	14
Daddy Day	8
Embarrassed	65
Field Trip	77
Fly Guy's Cinquain	109
Fly Guy's Senryu	111
Follow-the-Leader	32
Funny Time	64
Getting Out	54
Going	93

Good Morning	101
Grammar Lesson	49
Haiku	55
I Think I'll Leave My Snowsuit On	45
Laughing	104
Little Miss Moxie Day	9
Magic Show	89
Mama Day	8
Meathead	8
Mistletoe Millie	40
Mom!	33
Mr. Gold	112
Murphy Day	8
November 1st	29
On Halloween	24
Orville and Wilbur Wright	115
Ouch!	15
Our Dog	61
Paying Attention	56
Picture Day	62
Play Ball!	85
Poetry	103
Poetry Bug's Cinquain	109
Poetry Bug's Haiku	111

Running Away 71
Scary Costume 23
Sharing 22
Shoe Tying 78
Show and Tell 46
Super Spy 81
Thank You, Captain Cootie 80
The Artist 72
The First Day of Kindergarten 13
The Prank 47
The Rubber Band Game 88
The Store 21
The Train Name Game 94
The True Meaning of Christmas 38
Time to Go 95
Tomato Soup 86
We Could Have Bought a Hamster 102
What Really Happened to the Unicorns? 53
When Santa Came to School 39
Why Do I Have to Learn to Count Money? 37
Why Does the Moon Follow Me? 96

Poetry Bug Index

Alliteration	119
Assonant Rhyme	118
Bentley, E. Clerihew	113
Calligramme	117
Captain Cootie	120
Cinquain (form)	108
Cinquain (stanza)	107
Clerihew	113
Couplet	106
Crapsy, Adelaide	108
Double Dactyl	114
Emblematic Verse	117
Epigram	113

Figure Poem	117
Free Verse	112
Haiku	110
Hecht, Anthony	114
Lines	106
Mad Song Stanza	116
Pattern Poem	117
Perfect Rhyme/Assonant Rhyme	118
Quatrain	106
Senryu	111
Shape Poem	117
Sixain	107
Stanzas	106
Stress	114
Syllables	108
Triplet	106

Robert Pottle grew up in Eastport, Maine. He started writing poems to share with his first grade students. He now shares his poetry with children around the world with his web sites. Pottle also enjoys performing his poetry at schools and festivals. He now lives in Eastbrook, Maine, with his wife, children, and two llamas.

Jonathan Siruno was born in Warren, Michigan, in 1977 and moved to Maine at the tender age of six. To help fit in, Jon took up copying comic strips and cartoons. When he was 15, his real desire to do art hit while attending a summer art program at Pratt University. He furthered his education at the Savannah College of Art and Design, where he majored in Sequential Art - drawing funnybooks in lay terms. He has worked on several graphic novel anthologies. Jon now lives in Massachusetts.

To order a copy of MOXIE DAY and Family by mail, print this page and send along with $9.95 plus $1.99 shipping and handling to:

Blue Lobster Press
Dept. A
RR1 Box 509
Eastbrook, ME 04634

Maine residents add 5% sales tax, which is $.50 for a single book.

Name_____

Address_____

_____

Town/City_____ State_____

Zip Code_____ E-mail_____

Number of Copies_____

Would you like a signed copy? ___ Yes ___ No

If yes, who should it be signed to?_____

Make check or money order payable to: Blue Lobster Press. Checks must be drawn from a U.S. bank.

You can read more poetry by Robert Pottle, or even hear him recite his poetry on the popular web site *Giggle, Giggle, Snicker, Laugh!*

Visit *Giggle, Giggle, Snicker, Laugh!* on the internet at:

http://www.robertpottle.com

Visit Moxie Day on the internet at:

http://www.moxieday.com

Visit Blue Lobster Press at:

http://www.bluelobsterpress.com